STEP UP!

HOW TO BE AN EXCELLENT
ASSOCIATION BOARD MEMBER

ELIZABETH BAILEY

NANCY SCHMIDT

LATITUDE 33 PUBLISHING

Latitude 33 Publishing
1201 Morningside Drive, Suite 105
Manhattan Beach, CA 90266

Editor: Betsey Binét
Design: Gretchen Goetz

ISBN 978-0-9907349-0-1

Library of Congress Control Number: 2015960077

Printed in the United States of America
10 9 8 7 6 5 4 3 2 1

This book is dedicated to
the individuals who step up every day
to help lead their organizations.
You are truly the embodiment of pioneering
anthropologist Margaret Mead's call:
"Never doubt that a small group of
thoughtful, committed citizens can change the world;
indeed, it's the only thing that ever has."

Thank you to our wonderful families, friends,
colleagues, clients and creative team for
consistently demonstrating the meaning of excellence.

Table of Contents

Here's to stepping up!

On the scale of doing things in your lifetime that matter, serving on a board ranks way up there. It's an honor. And it's a tremendously important job with far-reaching implications. In fact, in *Engaged and On Board*, a national study we conducted of more than 1,200 nonprofit board members across the country, a resounding 85% agreed that their board service has helped them make a bigger impact than any other type of volunteering they have done.

Along with the great sense of satisfaction that comes from "doing good," board members overwhelmingly identified two major personal benefits:

- 95% made important new relationships
- 92% gained new skills

And the good news for those who are joining boards is that 84% have found the experience to be even better than they had expected.

It's an honor.

And it's a tremendously

important job

with far-reaching

implications.

It's a big job. Beyond the personal rewards you may gain from board membership, you are being entrusted with a very real, very important responsibility. Your actions tangibly impact the lives of many other important people: those who work or volunteer for the organization as well as those whom the organization exists to serve.

We have been privileged to devote much of our careers to the social-change sector. The following pages contain insights we've gained from many hours in board rooms and with staff, witnessing the highs and the lows, facilitating meaningful discussions and helping to guide organizations to new levels of engagement, impact and excellence. **We hope these insights will help you make the most of your board experience.**

As a **board member,**

your priority is the

association as a whole.

Wear the right hat.

The path to board service is reached in different ways. Perhaps you were elected by your fellow association members or appointed by a particular region or group. Or you were tapped by the board president or chief executive. Regardless of the road you traveled to get here, once you begin your board tenure, it's time to be sure you're wearing the proper gear: your association hat.

So what does that mean?

The organization will undoubtedly benefit from your unique perspective. But that's just one part of a bigger equation. As a board member, your priority is the association as a whole.

On the surface, this may seem obvious. However, too often board members believe that their role is to "represent" a certain perspective or a particular audience. Such a mindset can lead to a personal opinion or a special interest exerting a disproportionate influence on board-level decision making, which can have a negative impact on the overall organization.

As a board member, you have assumed the role of *steward*. As a steward, you are charged with ensuring that the organization is empowered to fulfill its mission on behalf of *all* members. Your job is to review and synthesize information thoughtfully, ask questions, engage in constructive debate and arrive at informed decisions and solutions that clearly align with the association's mission.

It could be argued that it's not possible for every board decision to benefit all association members directly. And the point is certainly not to try to be everything to everyone. Rather, it is to consciously wear your association hat while looking through your unique lens to make decisions that support the organization's mission and its ability to achieve its strategic goals.

...consciously wear your association hat

while looking through your unique lens

to make decisions that

support the organization's mission...

"The strength of the team

is each individual member.

The strength of each member

is the team."

PHIL JACKSON

Play your position.

When you become a board member, it's sometimes difficult to know what position you're playing. It's not your home turf. You need to know who is responsible for what, what is and isn't off limits, and how hands-on you should be.

Why you're on the team

Looking at the big picture, as a board member your goals are to:

- Make sure the organization is financially well-run and has the resources needed to fulfill its mission and goals.
- Help set high-level policy and strategy.
- Be an informed, visible representative and advocate for the organization.
- Hire and empower a skilled chief executive who builds and leads an effective staff.

Would you accept a paying job
without knowing what
was expected of you?

Of course not!

Yet, as our national study of nonprofit
and association board members
revealed, only one-third believed that they
had been fully oriented to their new role and
understood what was expected of them.

SOURCE: ENGAGED AND ON BOARD 2015

What's not in your playbook

Many board members are experienced leaders, and that may be one reason you have been asked to serve. If so, you're probably used to calling the shots — deciding who will fill key roles, which products or services to offer, how to market and sell them. While your expertise is certainly valued, *running the association is not part of your board member job description.*

That's not to say that the board is completely distanced from the workings of the organization; it's that the board and the staff have their own assignments.

Know the rules of engagement

Make it a priority at the outset to become familiar with your board responsibilities, written and unwritten, and fully understand the meaning of the terms that are used in your organization.

Understanding the
nuances and norms for
your association will help
you be a savvy player,
which will go a long way
toward helping your team
stay in sync and equipped to win
on behalf of your organization.

As a starting point, here are some general baselines for what board and staff members typically do in key areas:

Operations: Staff members create the annual budget based on the overall strategic priorities of the association, and board members approve it. From there, staff develop and implement work plans under the guidance and management of the chief executive, who supplies reports to the board. Board member responsibilities are to ensure the information they receive is thorough and sufficient, and then carry out their specified fiduciary responsibilities.

Policy Making and Strategic Decisions: Initial ideas can come from staff or the board; however, the board vets and approves major strategic changes and key policy positions based on information that is provided by staff. Major strategic decisions include things such as entering into a new programmatic area or changing the organization's name. Implementation, such as designing programs, adding personnel or developing new materials, is then handled by staff.

What's the secret to a great Board Chair-Chief Executive relationship?

The advice commonly given to board chairs and chief executives is to lay out a clear, prescriptive list of tasks and functions for each role and stick to them, no matter what. More recently, convincing evidence around this pivotal relationship has revealed that in highly successful nonprofits, the lines of responsibility are actually more blurred. In fact, rigid adherence to boundaries can be a symptom of a lack of trust.

Research is finding that the strongest partnerships are developed through open dialogue and a flexible, ongoing process of give and take, in which both individuals continually learn and find ways to tap each other's unique strengths and interests, to better achieve the organization's goals.

SOURCE: STUDY BY MARY L. HILAND, PHD, 2005

Working with staff is a balancing act.

The more involved you are, the more likely you'll work directly with staff from your association. In fact, you may spend more one on one time working with staff on projects or committees than you do with the chief executive. And that can be tricky.

Staff are obliged to work with you in two different ways: Deferring to you as a strategic leader of the association and, on a more practical level, giving you assignments and direction in specific areas. Being mindful of this duality will help you establish and maintain collaborative and productive staff relationships to ensure you get what you need to be both a leader and a doer.

In most organizations, when a board member calls, it triggers someone on staff to jump — sometimes really high. That can put staff members in an awkward position: As much as they may want to help, it can also distract them from the tasks for which they're being held accountable. Being thoughtful about these requests will help keep these situations in check.

As you build staff relationships and develop mutual trust, it's imperative to remain "above board." **Some lines should never be crossed:**

- Engaging in off-the-record conversations about your fellow board members, the association or its chief executive.
- Leveraging relationships with staff to gain an "insider scoop."
- Assuming the role of staff advocate or sounding board for staff complaints. This can actually put the organization at risk legally. Such matters should be handled through formal human resource channels.
- Putting yourself in a position that could be interpreted as personally or professionally inappropriate.

Ultimately, as a leader of the association,

you also have a great opportunity to help create an organization that both attracts and retains high-caliber personnel. The way you interact with the association's staff can make a big difference in the quality of their experience. By helping them feel recognized and appreciated, and by being a true partner in carrying out the association's work,

you bring out the best in everyone.

It is vital that board
members understand
the spirit of the
strategic plan.

Strategic planning is
not a *pro forma* exercise.
It's an organized, efficient
and systematic process for
charting a course for strategic
growth. When done well,
it is the catalyst for taking
your association to new
levels of effectiveness,
impact and success.

Go from Where?...
to There!

In some circles, the mere mention of "strategic planning" is met with yawns and eye rolls. It's viewed as a tedious process, yielding a document that, upon completion, is already irrelevant.

Actually, solid strategic planning is just the opposite. **It's a highly efficient, engaging, energizing process that gets everyone concretely on the same page.** Strategic planning enables the board and staff to take stock of where the association is today, creatively explore and identify future possibilities, define where it wants to be within a period of time (typically three years), and spell out how the organization will get there.

As a board member, strategic planning is one of your most propitious opportunities to help shape the organization and its impact, and guide your own involvement efforts.

Your role is to:

- **Ensure that your association has a plan.**
  A plan is essential, because it serves as the touchstone for key organizational decisions as well as the basis for staff work plans. A strategic plan also provides evidence to funders that your organization has its act together — in other words, it has a clear destination and a roadmap for getting where it wants to be.

- **Help inform the plan.** A few productive ways you can engage in the planning process are by participating in planning sessions and contributing your ideas through interviews and/or surveys. In some cases, a planning task force may be created; in others, the entire board may be actively involved. Regardless, there should be opportunities throughout the planning process for you to provide input before it is submitted for board approval.

■ **Actively support the plan's implementation.**
The work doesn't stop once the strategic plan is
completed. In fact, that's when the real action begins.
The board has an important role in helping to carry the
plan forward. Highly effective boards take this charge
seriously and ensure that each board member develops
his or her own annual personal impact plan that aligns
with the organization's strategic goals.

■ **Model accountability.** A well-conceived strategic plan
sets the stage and direction for measureable progress.
Expecting timely progress updates to the board from staff
is a given. It's equally important for the board to check in
on how its members are doing in relation to their personal
impact plans and to provide the support, encouragement
and recognition to keep everyone — staff and board
members — focused, engaged and productive.

■ **Evaluate and evolve.** In your role as a board member, a recurring question in much of your decision-making should be, "How will doing this help us achieve the goals in our strategic plan?" A well-constructed plan provides a clear framework for evaluating and pursuing new opportunities — or for cutting bait on strategies that are no longer working. Having a plan doesn't mean you stop thinking or become rigid. It does mean you stay true to the course and help the plan continue to evolve.

Ultimately, an effective strategic plan is essential for the organization.

It helps both the overall board and you as an individual focus your energy and commitment on the areas where you can make the greatest difference.

Make connections
not deals

Being on the lookout for new opportunities to advance your association, financially or otherwise, is commendable. Just bear in mind that in most situations, you're still more of a connector than a deal maker.

It is not uncommon for companies or other organizations to approach board members to gain an "in" with the association. They may chat you up at a conference, offer to take you to lunch or dinner, or invite you to a round of golf. Before you accept any invitations, it's best to check in with the chief executive or appropriate staff to get the lay of the land. If it's an entity that is of interest to your association, you'll want to ensure that you're in step with an overall strategy.

Unless it's been agreed to ahead of time, board members do not have the authority to state the association's potential interest in a partnership or commit the association to anything on their own. So until you've had an opportunity to speak with the chief executive, tread lightly.

Be a connector.

Among the many hats you wear as a board member is that of ambassador, or connector, for the association. In fact, you could say it's your most important role outside the boardroom.

Highly effective board members fully embrace being a public face for the association. They view this role as an enjoyable opportunity rather than a remote task relegated to the board chair and staff.

Being a good ambassador means taking stock of what you know and don't know about the association and filling in the gaps. It means staying on top of what's happening and participating in as many activities as your schedule allows. And it means engaging in a little personal reflection to gain clarity about why you personally believe the association has value.

Association board members can truly have an impact on membership recruitment and retention and on overall member engagement. You can be an outstanding ambassador by proactively finding opportunities to connect personally with current and potential members face-to-face, online or through the mail. In doing so, you'll be helping the association to:

■ Keep its fingers on the pulse of what's happening in the field.

■ Make new connections and identify potential new members.

■ Make a memorable and positive first impression.

■ Get the word out about member programs, benefits and new offerings.

■ Resolve any questions or misperceptions about the association.

■ Create a more personal experience for members and foster their sense of belonging.

Excellent ambassadors take note when something good has happened to a member or prospective member. They may send a personal note or email on behalf of the association recognizing the member's achievement.

Helping to increase visibility and appreciation for the association

can be one of the most rewarding aspects of serving on the board.

Being a good ambassador keeps you connected

and constantly reinforces why you've stepped up to help lead the association as well as the profession or industry it supports.

Relevance matters.
**Make sure your proof points
are as relatable as possible
to your audience.**

An easy mistake to make
**is talking about how wonderful
it is to be a board member
without giving examples that will
resonate with "regular" members.**

Take your elevator speech to a higher level.

Board members often say they're stumped when asked to explain their association in a succinct and compelling way to others. The usual default is to rattle off a reference to its size or longevity, recite a laundry list of benefits or make general comments about the great opportunities for networking — all of which can quickly fall on politely deaf ears. The second default is to ask staff to provide them with a ready-made elevator speech, which also typically falls flat.

Why? Because the magic in an elevator speech is authenticity — your personal proof points.

The fact is, you're not actually making a speech. You're giving someone a glimpse into your experience with the association in a way that is aimed at piquing their interest and opening the door to more conversation. **The response you are aiming for** is not, "Sounds like a good organization," but "Interesting... tell me more!"

Many of the well-established core components of an elevator speech are sound and should definitely be followed:

- Keep it short.
- Emphasize why the association exists (who it serves, why it's different).
- Convey its value (this is where your proof points come in).
- Practice and get comfortable, so the words will flow naturally at a moment's notice.

More about proof points

Neuroscientists can see it happening: People's brains light up when they are learning something new, when they are being prompted to see or do something differently than they have before, or when they are listening to an engaging story. You can trigger that response when you give a relevant and authentic account of how your association has positively changed something in your life.

It's immensely powerful when you go beyond simply describing a member benefit that your association offers — even in glowing terms — to giving a specific, personal story of how that service or benefit has actually altered an outcome for you or a fellow member.

That's when your association shifts from being something that's **"nice to have"** to something that's **"essential to have."**

Generic statement	Proof point
"They're our voice on Capitol Hill."	"Our legislative team is on top of it and was at the table when recent legislation was drafted. That helped open up new sources of funding that I've been able to tap for my school."
"I've met great people."	"At their last conference I met a fellow member who's been dealing with exactly the same issues as me. Having that conversation has changed my approach and saved me thousands of dollars."
"Membership includes professional liability/wrongful termination insurance."	"When everyone else in her department lost their jobs, my friend was the only one not terminated, and that was directly because of the legal support she received through this association."

When it comes to proof points, remember…

The more specific the better.

**Keep asking yourself, why would this matter
to the person I am talking to?**

**DON'T stop at the obvious –
keep digging until you strike gold!**

How can you identify your proof points?

Pause and ask yourself a few questions.
How has this association:

- Made my life easier?
- Saved me time, money or headaches?
- Made me look good to my staff or colleagues?

Periodically asking yourself those questions is a great habit to get into for a couple of reasons:

- You will keep collecting nuggets that can be used in conversations with others.
- You will also regularly remind yourself of the association's value. And that can continuously recharge your enthusiasm and commitment.

EXCELLENCE

STRIVE FOR EXCELLENCE,
NOT PERFECTION.

Excellence or perfection — why choose? Both excellence and perfection are admirable qualities. However, as it turns out, organizational psychologists have studied this topic extensively and concluded that the quest for perfection, while noble in theory, can create big stumbling blocks to getting things done in an organization.

It's worth taking a moment to reflect on this, because it defines a mindset that can increase your effectiveness as a board member.

EXCELLENCE

PERFECTION PERFECTION PERFECTION PERFECTION PERFECTION PERFECTION PERFECTION PERFECTION PERFECTION PERFECTION PERFECTION PERFECTION PERFECTION PERFECTION PERFECTION PERFECTION PERFECTION PERFECTION PERFECTION PEREFE PERFECTION PERFECTION PERFECTION PERFECTION PERFECTION PERFECTION PERFECTION PERFECTION PERFECTION PERFECTION PERFECTION PERFECTION PERFECTION

Here are a few telling comparisons:

Perfectionists	Excellence seekers
Set impossible goals	Set high and achievable goals
Are plagued by doubt	Are confident
Feel pressure	Feel excitement
Become overwhelmed and give up when they run into difficulty	Perceive setbacks as temporary and keep going
Are highly risk-averse	Are willing to take risks
Hate criticism and are devastated by failure	View criticism and failure as opportunities to learn
Need to have full control	Embrace spontaneity
Need to be Number One — or else	Find fulfillment in trying their hardest

Most of us have witnessed situations in which the compulsion to make every detail perfect or to control for every unknown has stalled group momentum, built frustration and caused an association to miss out on important opportunities.

Excellence, not perfection, holds the key.

EXCELLENCE

Seeking perfection is a solitary job.

Pursuing excellence is a way
to invigorate a group.

As a board member, you can contribute to a culture

of excellence: First, by putting your efforts into making
sure that high standards are set and issues are thoughtfully
considered; and second, by recognizing that you will never
have all the answers and will be continually testing and
learning along the way.

So, encourage your board to put its best foot

forward and go!

Give more than you take.

Serving on a board can be a heady experience.
You're on the inside. You may even be there because you've run for elective office and won. As historians and observers of human nature throughout time have told us, an unintended consequence of gaining power is its potential to elevate the ego and bring out a subtle (or not-so-subtle) sense of entitlement.

While the odds are low that you joined your board aspiring to be a supreme dictator or to have your ego stroked, it's deceptively easy to adopt habits or behaviors that subconsciously work against the true spirit of supporting your association.

A few self-serving scenarios to avoid:

Viewing the board as your personal soapbox. No matter how passionate or informed you are about an issue, a board meeting is not the place to pontificate. You and your colleagues will find it far more helpful to approach meetings with the goal of contributing your insights thoughtfully and efficiently to advance the identified agenda.

Siphoning off resources for pet projects. It's true that an enthusiastic champion is often key to a project or activity's success. Yet there can be pitfalls. A classic example is following a tradition in which board presidents select a theme or focus area for the year based on their personal interests. Too often, the type of project that results is more of a "one-off" than an opportunity to put more muscle into achieving a mission-critical goal. So take care that whatever idea you put forth or embrace is firmly aligned with the association's goals and strategic priorities.

Consuming significant, often scarce, resources. It can be extremely valuable to take a realistic look at how much of your association's human and financial resources are spent supporting governance functions. In long-standing associations, it's not uncommon for the board, committees, task forces and special-interest groups to balloon in size, becoming disproportionally heavy consumers of the association's resources. What often goes unrecognized is the staff time and resources that are required for every meeting, whether virtual or face-to-face: arranging logistics, juggling multiple schedules, creating background materials and talking points, prepping for presentations and conducting post-meeting follow-up. In addition, in-person meetings often entail direct costs for travel, lodging and food.

So before recommending yet another meeting or committee, think carefully about whether it is truly justified. You may find that simply by asking the question, you and your fellow board members may arrive at a better and more efficient way to advance an issue or project.

If you're in tune with where
your association's resources
are being spent,
you're much more likely
to make solid, informed
requests and decisions.

Balancing board perks

One of the key ways associations demonstrate appreciation for their board members is by holding meetings or retreats in enjoyable settings, offering interesting activities that facilitate relationship-building or giving tokens of appreciation to board members. These are usually heartfelt gestures, and it's appropriate to accept them graciously. Just make sure you and your fellow board members are doing your part to ensure that things don't become too extravagant.

"Life expands
or shrinks in
proportion to
one's courage."

ANAÏS NIN

COURAGE.
BRING IT!

Leading an association in today's hypercompetitive, rapidly changing world is not for the faint of heart. **It takes courage to face facts,** identify challenges and do something about them — especially if that means adopting bold, new approaches that break with long-held mindsets or traditions.

Courageous leadership means understanding and confronting realities, not denying them or putting off facing and addressing them. It means being willing to ask honest, open questions, gather objective data, and challenge "what we've always done" in the context of what genuinely needs to change, to ensure that the association fulfills its purpose.

There's a crucial difference
between bravery and courage.
While the brave take risks
and plunge into the unknown
without hesitation,
the courageous fully understand
the risks before them and
mindfully take action anyway,
despite their fears, in order to
achieve an end they believe in.

A courageous leader fully claims his or her leadership roles and responsibilities while fostering a culture of respect and collaboration. A courageous leader also recognizes that there are times when difficult or even unpopular decisions must be made and is willing to take on the uncomfortable task of leading the association through them. As mistakes are inevitably made, it takes another dose of courage to avoid pointing the finger at others, and instead accept responsibility, regroup and forge ahead.

Courage-infused leadership isn't always pretty, but the rewards are great. Courageous leadership builds credibility and trust. When you are recognized as a person of character, it's easy for others to believe in you and your cause.

By your willingness to serve on a board, you've shown that you are committed to making a difference. At times, that will mean digging deep and finding the courage to do what it takes to help transform the association.

"If we were supposed to talk
more than we listen,
we would have two tongues
and one ear."

MARK TWAIN

Listen up!

How many times have you waited impatiently for a fellow board member to stop talking so you can make your point? It happens all the time in board meetings, especially if the topic is highly charged or hotly debated.

We often overlook what someone is saying because **we're busy formulating a response**. Or as Stephen R. Covey notes in *The 7 Habits of Highly Effective People,* "Most people do not listen with the intent to understand; they listen with the intent to reply."

The eye roll.

The tapping foot.

The heavy sigh.

If you're guilty of one or all of these, you're sending a clear message to the person who's speaking: "I'm finished listening to you." Regardless of what they're saying or how they're saying it, be mindful of the message you're conveying as you listen. Everyone has his or her own opinions and individual manner of speaking. The boardroom is the perfect place to model respect and good listening skills.

Are you a sentence-grabber?

When impatience takes over, it's tempting to try to speed things along by interrupting a speaker or finishing others' sentences. Beyond disrupting the flow of information, the "interrupter" is following his or her own train of thought, squelching the opportunity to learn where the speaker was originally headed — and possibly sabotaging a great idea.

The International Listening Association estimates that we listen at the rate of 125-250 words a minute, but we think at 1,000-3,000 words a minute. With all those words vying for attention in our brains, it's a wonder we hear anything at all. By giving more air time to the words in our head than the ones entering our ears, we run the risk of missing something important, even vital. Turning down our own inner dialogue allows us to listen more fully and stay present and focused on the issue at hand.

The ability to give our full attention to what someone is saying is a profoundly important skill for board members. It takes practice, and isn't always easy. Being a good listener helps avoid misunderstandings and makes decision-making processes flow more smoothly. Good listening reinforces trust, strengthens relationships and makes a board's work more efficient, productive and meaningful.

Genuine listening not only helps everyone better understand a situation or issue; it will help you and your fellow board members get the firmest possible grip on the best ways to address your association's needs.

When you see diversity in the boardroom, you're in good company!

Social physics research by MIT's Media Lab and other studies reveal that groups with a mix of ages, genders and cultural backgrounds regularly come up with more effective and feasible solutions than those that are homogeneous.

There's more to diversity than meets the eye.

Diversity has a multitude of facets — some we're born with, some we've picked up along the way — and they all help to define us. Every individual brings a rich combination of assets to the table. Common traits and experiences can be a basis for bonding, while those that are different have the potential to expand one's thinking.

As a board member, it's critical to remember that diversity goes far beyond the observable demographics of age, gender, race and ethnicity. The term also applies to all of the possibilities along the various dimensions of occupation, educational background, income, religious and political beliefs, hometown, sexual orientation/gender identity, marital and parental status, and so on.

Diversity is no longer a concept: It's our reality.

The long-predicted tectonic shifts in demographics are upon us. One key indicator of how quickly times are changing: As recently as 1990, the U.S. population was more than 75 percent Caucasian. However, those born after 2003 are the vanguard of the first majority-minority generation in our history, in which no ethnic group will approach 50 percent. This cohort fully expects to be immersed in diversity and views anything else as off-kilter.

SOURCE: US CENSUS BUREAU

How do excellent board members think about diversity?

They seek it and embrace it. There's growing scientific evidence that considering diverse points of view not only leads to more creative and innovative thinking, but richer relationships. So actively look for ways to include board members from across the spectrum of opinions, values and backgrounds that exist in your association.

They pay attention to differences but don't overgeneralize. Broad assumptions surface in boardrooms all the time – for instance, when a board member turns to a Latino colleague and asks how Catholics feel about an issue, never considering that might not be his religion. While it is appropriate to consider the cultural context of your fellow board members, at the same time it's just as important to stop short of stereotyping and assuming all members of a particular group feel and act exactly the same way.

"Diversity is the art
of thinking independently
together."

MALCOLM FORBES

Each recognizes that he or she is not the sum of their demographic. On the flip side, if you're the only person under 30 in the room, resist the temptation to speak as the definitive voice for your entire generation. While you certainly have useful insights, the way you really add value is by helping your colleagues see nuances they might miss and connecting them with others in your age group who can expand their experience.

They keep an open mind and strive to avoid judging or dismissing other perspectives. As entrepreneur and publisher Malcolm Forbes observed, "Diversity is the art of thinking independently together."

They get more data when it's needed. One person does not a trend make. To identify trends, you need a broader perspective. When key strategic decisions are being contemplated, it's critical that you use good, objective data obtained from key audiences outside the boardroom.

Alphabet-soup acronyms and jargon

plague most associations.

As a board member, it's important

for you to take ownership by learning

what all those letters stand for.

You might suggest that staff maintain

a working "code list"

of key terms to help everyone

stay on the same page.

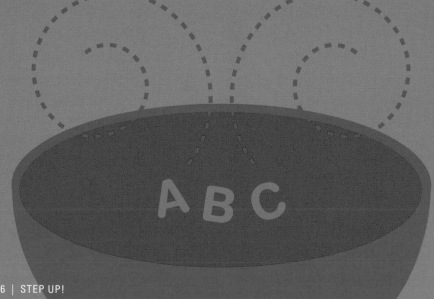

Do your homework.

It's always challenging to find your balance among work, home and volunteer activities. And without a doubt, adding "board member" to your list of roles includes a certain amount of outside-the-boardroom homework. It's a very real part of the job.

In advance of each board meeting, staff typically work diligently to prepare and distribute board packets that give all the detailed information you'll need to participate in focused deliberations, pose insightful questions and arrive at sound decisions.

So read them!

Too often, reviewing pre-meeting materials can become a last-minute exercise — sometimes so last-minute that you're literally sitting in the room just seconds before the meeting begins before you crack open the packet and furiously thumb through it.

Those who do not take the time to review information thoughtfully before a meeting often find themselves in a precarious position: They either bog down the meeting by asking questions about topics that are clearly covered in the materials; or their embarrassment at being unprepared gets the best of them, and they blindly vote with the majority. Neither does justice to your role or the association.

Here's another benefit to advance preparation: Say you have received information ahead of time, but you aren't sure how to read and interpret a financial report or some other component. Excellent! Now you have time before the meeting to reach out and get clarification from staff, so you **come to the meeting confident, prepared and ready to move the association forward.**

Avoid the three Ds: Distraction, Disruption, Downer.

It's the little things that can wreak havoc on group dynamics and derail meetings. Recognizing and steering clear of behaviors that undermine your board's effectiveness and send meetings careening into the ditch is a responsibility that each board member can and should fully own.

Brain research shows

that if you lead with a positive statement,
your comments stand a much better chance
of being accepted by others.

"THE NEUROCHEMISTRY OF POSITIVE CONVERSATIONS"
BY JUDITH GLASER AND RICHARD GLASER,
HARVARD BUSINESS REVIEW, 2014

So... when possible, start by noting an
aspect of the idea you genuinely like. If
that's not feasible, you can express your
appreciation of the work that has gone into
researching the topic, or how important
you think it is to bring ideas to the table.
From there, you can air specific questions or
concerns. The goal is to arrive at a solution
that works, not simply to tank what's being
discussed and considered.

Distractors engage in sidebar conversations, constantly check their email or mobile devices, or do something other than actively listen and participate in the meeting.

It's one thing to make a friendly aside or comment to the person next to you. Just make it quietly, and keep it brief. Conducting a full-on conversation, searching online to validate or invalidate something that has been said means you're actually conducting a separate meeting.

Disrupters lob toxic, verbal grenades into the boardroom. Their vehemently stated opinions suck the energy out of the room, put people on the defensive, and can make some feel too intimidated to speak up. This is especially true if the boardroom bully or know-it-all is a longtime member, and others are new to the scene.

> **"That's the stupidest idea I've ever heard."**
> **"That will never work."**
> **"Sheesh... We tried this a few years ago, and it failed miserably. Why are we wasting time on it now?"**

When statements are loaded with emotion and delivered with authority, those who feel less strongly may refrain from voicing their own more balanced opinions. On the other hand, those who strongly disagree may join in with equally incendiary, counterproductive remarks. Dominating a meeting is a surefire way to shut down honest input and discussion.

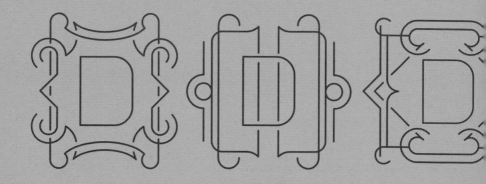

"Be an appreciator, not a depreciator."

DR. WAYNE W. DYER

Downers make being critical or playing devil's advocate their default mode. Their first instinct is to "go to the dark side" and reject an idea out of hand. Instead of considering positive possibilities, their primary focus is to reveal why something doesn't or won't work.

Downers may position themselves as the voice of reason with superior experience or organizational knowledge. It can become part of their identity to believe that, by taking on the role of resident critic, they are serving as a "protector" of the association.

Even well-intentioned actions of this type can stymie a group's ability to engage in meaningful discussion, productively challenge conventional thinking and contribute ideas and solutions.

What to do about a really bad idea?

If you think an idea is flawed, you have a responsibility to speak up. But resist the urge to blurt out a scathing criticism. It will make a difference if you pause, breathe deeply and take a moment to frame your thoughts. Make it your job to bring positive energy into the boardroom.

NO ELEPHANTS
OR COWS.

"Are we going to talk about
the elephant in the room?"

With long histories and multiple stakeholders, **associations
are fertile ground for invisible elephants and sacred
cows.** Both become particularly problematic in the boardroom,
where a put-everything-on-the-table mode of operating is
essential to ensure that the association focuses resources on
what matters most to members and supports activities that
truly deliver a solid return on investment.

It's not uncommon for research or a strategic-planning process
to turn up activities or organizational artifacts that are out
of alignment with the association's mission or are draining
resources that are disproportionate to the value they deliver.

Adhering to a

no-elephants-and-sacred-cows

policy plays an important role in

maintaining a board culture

that fosters trust,

open communication and creative

problem-solving.

For example, governance structures and processes may have become unwieldy. Pet programs may have continued "just because." And other association activities may still be in place despite declining interest and usage.

It can feel personal. A sacred cow could be something that is truly beloved by a handful of tenured and respected leaders or a subgroup of constituents. The "elephant in the room" could be a major initiative that is not succeeding as expected. Shifting strategy or cutting bait can be complicated, even embarrassing. However, regardless of the situation or scenario, ignoring the issue will do nothing to help the association.

In truth, being timid in the boardroom can have serious repercussions. By the time the sense of urgency builds to raise questions or suggest that something may need to change, it can be too late — after the association has already slid into crisis mode or missed important opportunities. Attempting to manage sensitive issues from a defensive or reactive position almost always results in damaged relationships and less-than-desired outcomes.

"If you always do

what you've always done,

you'll always get

what you've always got."

HENRY FORD

How to contend with these animals?

The first step is to make it safe to bring them out into the open. Any board member can set that in motion, starting with something as simple as an acknowledgment that every organization has them, and that it's part of the work of the board to look at them periodically with clear, custodial eyes. Doing so opens the door for proactive discussions that can be handled in a respectful manner that honors past decisions while staying focused on making whatever changes are called for, and keeps the association relevant and successfully moving forward.

"Where all think alike,
no one thinks very much."

WALTER LIPPMANN

"Honest disagreement
is often a good sign of progress."

MOHANDAS K. GANDHI

CONFLICT

IS NOT A DIRTY WORD.

There are lots of reasons why we are conditioned to shy away from conflict in a group. Conflict can make us uncomfortable. It can feel hostile. It's perceived to create winners and losers. It can cause rifts that damage relationships. **For most people, conflict sits on the opposite side of fun;** people regularly describe themselves as being conflict-averse.

Yet, in groups of diverse people with passionately held beliefs and opinions, **conflict is both natural and inevitable.** In fact, it is often through conflict — or working through differing beliefs and opinions — that some of the biggest, most promising opportunities emerge.

As a board member, how do you deal most effectively with "Conflict"?

Expect conflict and recognize the valuable potential it holds. When you sense dissension coming, remember that allowing deep-seated feelings to surface can create the opportunity to air issues that may be holding back the work of the board. By dispensing with superficial politeness and directly addressing differences, you can reach new levels of honesty, trust and relationship-building.

Be prepared for it. Make sure you understand the protocol for how your board handles serious differences of opinion. Whose role is it to take charge? What processes are in place to make sure the issue is managed respectfully and productively? If a clear, transparent process doesn't exist, consider suggesting that the board articulate one.

Be curious. Before you jump in with a vocal opinion or dig in your heels, challenge yourself to explore what different pieces of information or experiences may be contributing to the disparate perspectives around the table. This is your chance to gain valuable knowledge and show genuine interest in other vantage points and, at the same time, help diffuse emotions.

Use your insights to arrive at a new and better place together. "Compromise" is not a dirty word, either. In fact, it's often the key to productive conflict resolution. Considering multiple possibilities and encouraging divergent thinking builds the muscles that can help your board become a more finely-tuned working team that is not only able to make effective day-to-day decisions, but capable of coming up with breakthrough ideas.

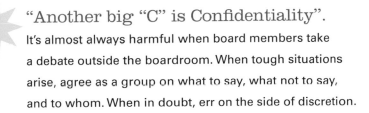

"Another big "C" is Confidentiality".
It's almost always harmful when board members take a debate outside the boardroom. When tough situations arise, agree as a group on what to say, what not to say, and to whom. When in doubt, err on the side of discretion.

Boards only have
authority as a group,
not as individuals.

Stand as one.

Boards exist in part to make substantive decisions,
from setting an association's strategic direction and goals to
hiring the chief executive and approving the annual budget.
In each case, boards are called upon to review, deliberate and
arrive at informed decisions that align with and support the
association's mission.

Although a board is composed of individuals, it only has
authority as a group. **Each and every board member
is bound by the decisions that the board makes
collectively.**

It's expected that not every decision will receive unanimous
approval and support. In fact, there may be heated debates
and strong opposing positions. However, once an issue
receives the required votes to approve it, kill it, or send it
back for further review, it becomes a decision that the entire
board must own.

What happens

in the boardroom

stays in the

boardroom.

When opinions differ, deliberations need to occur within the structure of the board rather than outside it. It can be extremely damaging to an organization for board members to air their dissatisfaction or concerns to constituents, staff or the media. Regrettably, individuals sometimes attempt to justify rogue actions as a personal "CYA" strategy, to warn someone about what's happening, or to lay the groundwork for an I-told-you-so moment. Being publicly at odds with collective board decisions, including having off-the-record discussions with staff or others, is almost never in the best interest of the association, and it can actively undermine the chief executive's ability to lead effectively.

Tough decisions come with the territory. Inevitably, you may find yourself opposed to a group decision. If the issue is big enough, it may be the catalyst for you to reassess your participation on the board. More likely, it will be an opportunity for you to stretch your leadership skills to view and understand the issue from a different perspective.

You can take heart in the fact that those who study organizations generally agree with oft-quoted entrepreneur Douglas Merrill: **"All of us are smarter than any of us."** And regardless of the circumstance, it is each board member's obligation to uphold confidentiality, to make decisions collectively and to speak with one voice.

When you change seats,

YOUR ROLE CHANGES, TOO.

Way to go! You've stepped up and have become the board chair, or you've agreed to head up a key committee or task force.

If this is a new role for you, the shift may feel a little unsettling at first.

Chances are, you're in this new leadership position because you've proved to be an engaged and effective board member with a passion for the mission, a strong personality and a penchant for getting things done.

That's all good. However, in this new position, your primary job is no longer to be your vocal, persuasive self. Instead, you are being called upon to manage the group's process. That means it's your responsibility to ensure that everyone is heard, that ideas and solutions are vetted and the work of the group gets done.

Create a board meeting that YOU would want to attend.

Take care of the real business. Make meaty topics the focus of the agenda; handle routine matters as succinctly and efficiently as possible.

Expand knowledge and understanding. Include programming by staff or outside experts that provides interesting and important insights into your association's sector, a particular program or area of focus, or how-to's to help your board perform at its highest level.

Inspire and motivate. Feature real examples and authentic stories that highlight the difference the association is making in the lives of those you serve. And always recognize and celebrate progress!

For someone who is used to being an active player, it takes some discipline to think of yourself as a facilitator, in charge of running a productive meeting. It also means thinking a few steps ahead to make sure everything moves along smoothly. To accomplish this, a little preparation goes a long way.

Work with the chief executive and staff to prepare a thoughtful and strategic agenda. Clearly identify the decisions that need to be made or the actions that need to be taken. Determine where gaps may exist in the board's understanding of key topics. Anticipate questions that will likely require answers. Make sure everyone has the necessary facts and context to make informed decisions. Build in time to recognize "wins" and progress. And remember to include a "mission moment" to help people stay connected to the meaningful work you're helping to accomplish.

You'll be glad you took the time to help inform the agenda, because an effective chairperson can truly make the difference between productive, successful, inspiring meetings and those that are a frustrating waste of time.

It's your responsibility to ensure
that everyone is heard, that ideas and solutions are vetted and that the work of the group gets done.

What will your legacy be?

As author and educator Steven Covey advises,
"Begin with the end in mind."
Embrace the association's strategic vision and direction,
and make some personal goals as you start out
that reflect the impact you would like to make
both during and after your board tenure.

Make a graceful exit.

**No matter how distant it may feel now, the day will
come when your service on the board is at an end.**

In the best case, leaving the board is part of the normal
course of events, with your term clearly delineated and
ending on schedule.

Or your departure could be precipitated by internal or external
events. Perhaps a substantive change has occurred within the
association that you're unable to stand behind. Or you've dug
deep and determined that, while worthy, the association isn't
honestly at or near the top of your volunteer commitment
priorities. Maybe something in your personal or professional
life is driving the need for a change.

Whatever leads up to that moment, you can do a lot to
orchestrate a positive transition for both you and the
association by applying a few basic principles:

- Do some advance planning.
- Be honest and transparent.
- Show courtesy and respect.

Be gracious.

Regardless of the circumstances, take the high road.
Express your gratitude and liberally extend compliments for
whatever you have found to be positive about your board
experience. Include as many people as you authentically can.

Facilitate a smooth handoff.

Create a transition plan for any activities you are leading
or for which you carry major responsibility. If you chair a
committee, or play a key role in specific events or activities,
provide your successor with the background, documents, plans
and budgets needed to carry it forward. If possible, personally
brief whoever will be taking on the task. Stay engaged until
the end, and actively participate in whatever formal process
has been established for wrapping up your service, helping to
identify and recruit your successor, or whatever is called for
through your board's protocol.

Share what you've learned.

Your reflections on your experience can be very useful
for those who will carry the association forward. A good
practice is for associations to conduct exit interviews with
departing board members. The formal, confidential setting
of this conversation affords a perfect opportunity to provide
candid feedback and constructive suggestions. If the
organization doesn't have such a process in place, consider
initiating a call or meeting with the chief executive and
the appropriate board leader.

If you want to stay involved – find a way!

Board members know more about the association than the vast majority of its constituents ever will. You're family. Former board members are often some of the association's most persuasive, effective ambassadors and supporters long after their official board service has come to a close. **Making it known that you are eager and willing to continue to play a meaningful role – in addition to continuing to be a supportive, active member – will make your exit all the more graceful and positive.**

"I've learned that
people will forget what you said,
people will forget what you did,
but people will never forget
how you made them feel."

MAYA ANGELOU

Being proactive is far better **than having someone else, however gently and diplomatically, ask you to bow out.** If you sense that you are not living up to your board responsibilities, it's likely that others have noticed too. Rather than staying in that uncomfortable void, take the initiative. Have a conversation with the chief executive and appropriate board leaders to determine the best possible course of action.

When a mid-course departure is called for...

Regardless of the reason, there are some ways to create a softer landing for yourself and everyone involved:

- **Make an honest assessment.** Identify the factors that are in play, and whether they are creating a short-term situation or a long-term problem. Then thoughtfully consider the pros and cons of staying – both for your own good and the good of the association.

- **As early as possible, involve the chief executive and appropriate board leaders.** Let them know what you are dealing with and get their perspectives on how best to handle things. Maybe you can continue in a modified way. Perhaps you need to phase out immediately or over a defined period. Or there might be another solution that you haven't thought of on your own.

- **Recognize how difficult it can be to let go of something you care about and probably enjoy.** That's where it helps to let your loyalty to the association come to the forefront, and make it your priority to do whatever is in its best interest.

GO
ALL
IN

What should you do now? **GO ALL IN.**

If you're going to make the most of your board service, this is no time to hold back. In that spirit, here are a few ideas:

- **Transform your passion for the profession or cause into full-on enthusiasm for the association.** People often connect with a cause first and an organization second. Try reshuffling that order, and recognize that focusing your energies on building a thriving association can actually help advance the cause or profession in which you believe, in far more substantial and sustainable ways than you could accomplish on your own.

- **Stretch beyond your comfort zone.** Be on the lookout for opportunities in which your talents, experience and connections can make a difference, including those that may lie beyond your usual wheelhouse.

- **Make every minute count.** Time is your most precious and limited commodity. So don't just spend it; invest it with intention and purpose where it will yield the biggest returns.

GO
ALL
IN

- **Walk your talk.** Being a board member sends a public signal that the association is deeply important to you. Giving to your capacity — in both time and talent — elevates your credibility as well as your impact.

In a nutshell...

Show up.

Never give up.

And whenever

the opportunity

presents itself —

STEP UP!

Resources

It's an exciting time in the social change sector, and a lot of great work is being done. A few of our favorite resources include:

ASAE – The Center for
Association Leadership
asaecenter.org

BoardSource
boardsource.org

BlueAvocado
blueavocado.org

The Bridgespan Group
bridgespan.org

The Goodman Center
thegoodmancenter.com

Integral, LLC
integral-dc.com

Knight Foundation
knightfoundation.org

Mary Byers, CAE
marybyers.com

Philanthropy 2173
philanthropy.blogspot.com

Stanford Social
Innovation Review
ssir.org

Sarah Sladek
xyzuniversity.com

techsoup
techsoup.org